Story Prompts
Horror

The Art of Writing Scary Stories

Created by Mark El-Ayat

For permission requests, write to the publisher, addressed "Attention: Permissions Coordinator," at the address below:

Mark El-Ayat Publishing
Email: Admin@markelayat.com
Website: Markelayat.com

Publisher logo:

Book cover by Mark El-Ayat

First Edition

ISBN: 979-8-9889467-3-1

Printed in United States of America

Year of Publication: 2024

Introduction

Welcome to Story Prompts Horror: The Art of Writing Scary Stories, your gateway into the chilling depths of horror writing. These pages are designed not just to spook and unsettle, but to explore the breadth and complexity of horror as a storytelling medium. Whether you're an aspiring horror writer or a pro wanting to explore the dark side, this book is made for you.

Horror uniquely binds us through shared fears, transcending boundaries by tapping into the universal dread of the unknown. This genre demands a blend of suspenseful tension and a profound understanding of human vulnerabilities. Here, we plunge into the craft of creating narratives that not only frighten but also provoke thought and stir the emotions.

This book offers a collection of prompts across a spectrum of horror subgenres, from supernatural to psychological horror, each designed to ignite your imagination and challenge your storytelling prowess. We also provide essential tools such as plot outlines and character development sheets to help you construct your stories with precision and depth. These resources serve as your foundation, supporting you as you build tales that are as compelling as they are terrifying.

By exploring various subgenres, you'll uncover the full scope of horror writing, learning to infuse terror and unease through stories of ghostly hauntings, apocalyptic visions, and eldritch horrors. Think of the prompts as doorways into the darkest corners of your creative psyche.

As you turn each page, remember that horror reflects life's darker side, its mysteries, and, crucially, its fears. Scary stories are all about revealing the creepy side of everyday life and finding terror in the smallest things.

So, arm yourself with a pen, steel your nerves, and open your mind to the shadows. The world can be a horrifying place, and it's writers like you who bring its darkest tales to light. Welcome to the gripping journey of writing scary stories.

Let the adventure begin!

Plot Outlines

When writing a horror story, it's crucial to capture the essence of fear. The workbook has different sections, like the Plot Outline template and Character Development sheet, to help you plan your bone-chilling story in detail. When you outline your story, make sure to create a clear and concise framework. Leave space to add all the creepy details and spooky stuff in the Notes section.

Plot Outlines are key to your horror story, giving you a roadmap to build suspense, terror, and resolution. It guarantees that your narrative grips readers with fear and darkness.

Within these pages, you will find a framework specially designed for the horror genre. The Plot Outline guides you through key stages of your story, from the unsettling start to the terrifying climax and, finally, the eerie resolution.

Use the Plot Outlines section to come up with a story that's both scary and emotionally captivating. Consider this section an invitation to carefully craft your story's journey, offering a comprehensive strategy for developing your horror narrative.

In horror writing, the utilization of the classic 3-act structure is particularly effective. This structure is famous for its ability to tell captivating stories. It splits the story into setup, escalation, and climax, making the tension and character development feel natural.

By using this structure skillfully, we can create a suspenseful and horrifying experience that will leave the reader thrilled and satisfied. This structure provides a clear pathway while also allowing the flexibility to explore the depths of horror, making it an ideal foundation for a wide array of horror stories.

Using this framework guarantees a cohesive and powerful horror storyline, evoking deep-seated fears in the audience and leaving a lasting impact on them.

Character Development

Character development is essential in crafting horror stories that truly terrify and captivate. These well-developed characters make your stories way scarier, drawing readers into a world where every shadow and whispered fear matters. These sheets in the workbook will help you dig deep into your main characters' minds, from their fears to their secrets, their vulnerable moments to their motivations. These investigations will not only reveal how your characters confront their nightmares but will also enrich your narrative with a genuine sense of dread and suspense.

Remember, the most compelling horror characters are those that resonate authentically with readers. They are flawed, they evolve, and they often face their deepest fears. If you take the time to really develop the characters, it sets the stage for a horror story that sticks with you.

In horror writing, the depth and complexity of your characters can elevate a simple scary scenario into a gripping, spine-chilling tale.

Characters are pivotal for delivering fear. This Character Development Sheet guides you in creating characters that not only resonate with horror but enhance the tension and atmosphere of your stories.

Basic Information: Start with the basics like name, age, occupation, and appearance to set the stage for your characters.

Backstory: Delve into your characters' pasts to unearth their darkest fears and secrets. A well-crafted backstory not only adds depth but also opens up avenues for psychological horror and personal stakes.

Personality Traits: Identify key traits that make your characters realistic and relatable. Are they skeptical, paranoid, or overly curious? Use these traits to drive their decisions and reactions in terrifying situations.

Goals and Motivations: What drives your characters? Their goals can lead them into the heart of darkness, whether they're seeking knowledge, redemption, or survival. Understanding these motivations is crucial for developing the plot and enhancing the horror.

Fears and Flaws: Horror thrives on vulnerability. Pinpoint their fears and flaws to craft scenes that test their limits and break their composure, heightening the horror of their journey.

Relationship Dynamics: The relationships between characters can be a source of tension and fear. Explore how these dynamics play out under stress, from family bonds tested by secrets to alliances formed under duress.

Character Arc: Horror characters often undergo significant transformations. Map out their journey from denial to acceptance, from fear to confrontation, ensuring their evolution is compelling and integral to the story's climax.

Dialogue Styles: Craft dialogue that reflects their fear and personality. How they speak can add layers to the atmosphere—whispered secrets, frantic warnings, or quiet resignations can all heighten the story's emotional impact.

This Character Development sheet is your tool to create characters that not only drive the horror forward but also connect deeply with readers, making your stories not just frightening but unforgettable.

Your journey into the dark begins here.

The Subgenres

Supernatural Horror

Supernatural horror ventures into the unsettling realm of the paranormal, where ghosts, demons, and other otherworldly entities breach the everyday world. This genre captivates with its exploration of the unknown, featuring haunted locales, spiritual possession, and eerie encounters. Supernatural horror combines ancient folklore with modern nightmares. These stories are not only thrilling, but they also make you think about what happens after we die and the unseen forces that surround us.

Key Elements:

- <u>Eerie Atmospheres:</u> Settings play a crucial role, with haunted houses, desolate landscapes, and other chilling locales providing a backdrop that enhances the sense of dread.

- <u>Paranormal Entities:</u> Ghosts, spirits, and demonic presences drive the conflict, challenging the characters' understanding of reality.

- <u>Psychological Impact:</u> The encounters often have profound psychological effects on the characters, blending terror with deep emotional and mental consequences.

Notable Works and Authors:

1. *The Haunting of Hill House* by Shirley Jackson: An occult scholar and his group experience terrifying supernatural occurrences in an old mansion determined to keep its secrets.

2. *The Shining* by Stephen King: A family's winter stay at an isolated hotel descends into a nightmare as supernatural forces influence the father, turning him against his own family.

3. *Hell House* by Richard Matheson: A team investigates the infamous Belasco House, only to find the malignant presence within challenging their sanity and survival.

4. *The Turn of the Screw* by Henry James: A governess encounters ghostly apparitions that threaten the children in her care, blurring the lines between reality and hallucination.

Writing Tips:

- **Build Suspense Gradually:** Let the fear grow slowly— subtle disturbances that escalate can often be more terrifying than overt horrors.

- **Focus on Mood and Tone:** Use detailed descriptions and sensory information to create an atmosphere that keeps readers on edge.

- **Play with Ambiguity:** Keeping readers questioning what's real and what might be the product of a character's imagination can heighten the sense of horror.

Plot Outline Template

Title: _____

Setting: _____

Theme: _____

Act 1: Setup

• Introduction to Characters: _____

• Inciting Incident: _____

• Establishing Stakes: _____

Key Elements:

• Establish the type of horror

• Initial terrifying conflict

Act 2: The Confrontation

• Deepening Complications: _____

• Midpoint: _____

• Build-Up to Crisis: _____

Key Elements:

• How does the horror evolve or escalate

• The introduction of secondary conflicts or subplots

Act 3: The Resolution

• Climax: _____

• Falling Action: _____

• Denouement/Conclusion: _____

Key Elements:

• Ensure all horrific conflicts are resolved. Stay consistent with the horror

• Highlight how characters have changed

Character Development Sheet

Character Names: _____ / _____

• Nicknames: _____ / _____

• Ages: _____ / _____

• Occupations: _____ / _____

• Physical Descriptions: _____ / _____

• Distinguishing Features (e.g., scars, tattoos):

_____ / _____

Backstory

• Family Background: _____ / _____

• Education & Career Path: _____ / _____

• Significant Past Events: _____ / _____

• Socioeconomic Status: _____ / _____

Personality

• Dominant Traits: _____ / _____

• Fears: _____ / _____

• Desires: _____ / _____

• Hobbies/Interests: _____ / _____

• Habits (good and bad): _____ / _____

• Values & Beliefs: _____ / _____

Relationships

• Current Family Dynamics: _____ / _____

• Friendships: _____ / _____

• Past Romantic Relationships: _____

Goals

• Personal Aspirations: _____ / _____

• Professional Ambitions: _____ / _____

• Romantic Desires: _____ / _____

Conflict

• Internal Conflicts (psychological struggles, fears, uncertainties):

_____

_____

• External Conflicts (with other characters, society, environment):

_____

_____

Character Arc

• Beginning State (personality, situation at the story's start):

_____

_____

• Growth Points (key moments of change):

_____

_____

• End State (transformation or realization by the end):

_____

_____

Dialogue Style

• Speech Patterns (formal, casual, idiosyncratic phrases):

_____ / _____

• Voice (how the character's personality is reflected in dialogue):

_____ / _____

Notes

The Prompt

A night watchman at an abandoned hospital encounters bizarre occurrences that hint at the tragic events once held within its walls. How does he confront these supernatural happenings?

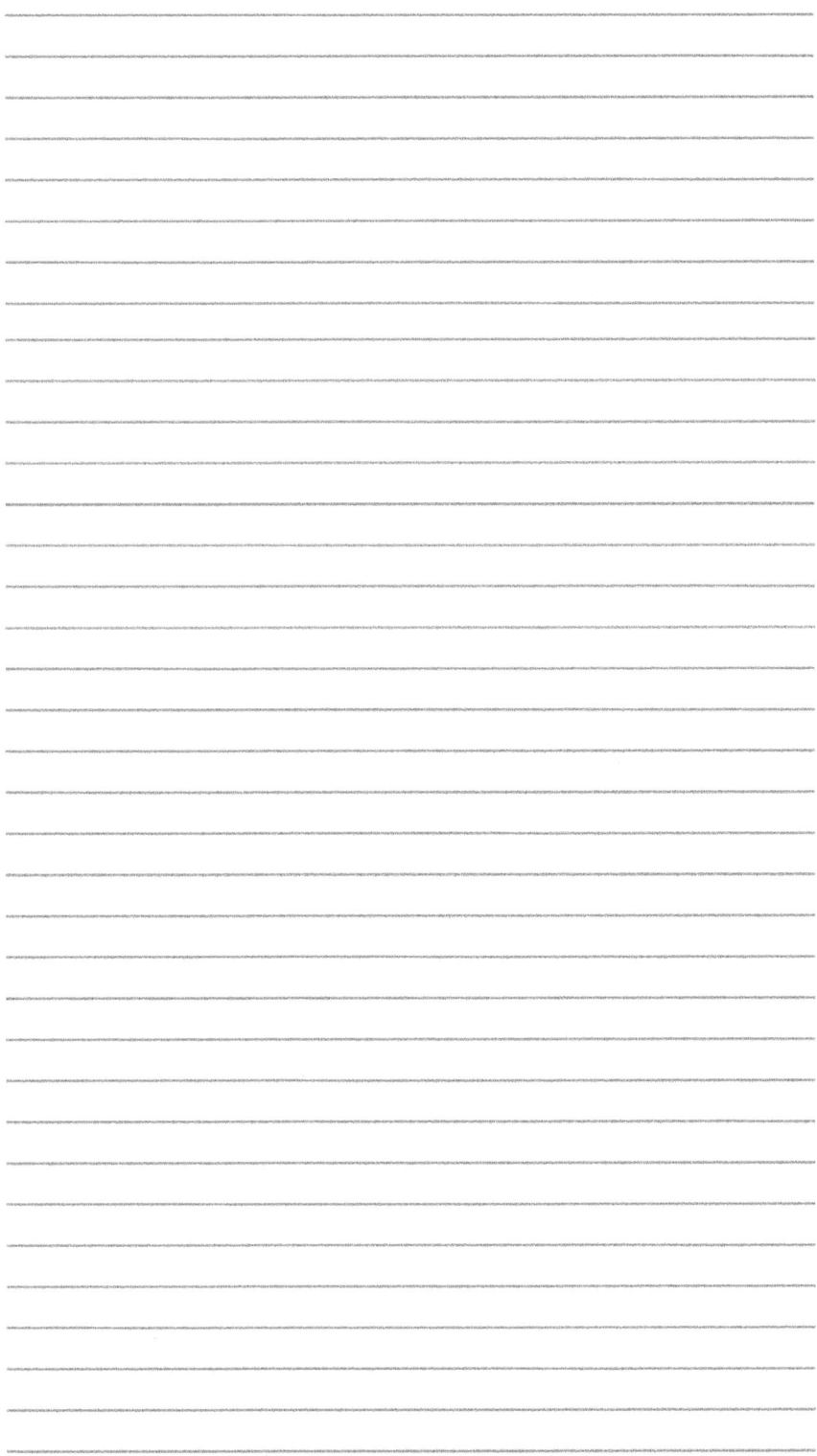

Psychological Horror

Psychological horror takes a deep dive into the human mind, delving into the unsettling aspects of mental instability, paranoia, and inner fears. This subgenre emphasizes the emotional and psychological states of characters, creating internal terror. In psychological horror, the distinction between reality and illusion becomes hazy, leading both characters and readers to question what is actually real. The horror lies in the mind's power to create fears as intimidating as physical threats, exposing the vulnerability of the human mind.

Key Elements:

- Unreliable Narrators: The use of characters who may not see the world clearly or whose judgment is clouded by fear or mental distress, adding layers of mystery and confusion.

- Manipulation of Perception: Stories that twist perception to make the ordinary seem terrifying, using psychological tricks to distort reality.

- Exploration of Fear: In-depth exploration of characters' deepest fears, phobias, and neuroses, which drive the narrative tension and horror.

Notable Works and Authors:

1. *The Silence of the Lambs* by Thomas Harris: An ambitious FBI trainee enlists the help of the infamous cannibalistic psychiatrist, Dr. Hannibal Lecter, to capture a serial killer known as Buffalo Bill, who skins his female victims.

2. *The Yellow Wallpaper* by Charlotte Perkins Gilman: A woman's prescribed "rest cure" in an isolated room leads to obsession and madness as she becomes entranced by the room's grotesque wallpaper.

3. *Misery* by Stephen King: An author becomes imprisoned by his "number one fan," experiencing psychological and physical torture that blurs lines between devotion and deranged obsession.

4. *Shutter Island* by Dennis Lehane: A U.S. Marshal's investigation at a psychiatric facility turns into a nightmarish quest for truth as his own mental stability is called into question.

Writing Tips:

- **Focus on Internal Conflict:** Develop the psychological complexity of characters to drive the narrative, emphasizing their internal conflicts and unstable emotional states.

- **Use Atmosphere to Enhance Fear:** Employ a claustrophobic, tense atmosphere that mirrors the characters' psychological states, intensifying the feeling of entrapment or disorientation.

- **Maintain Ambiguity:** Keep the readers guessing about the nature of the horror—what's real may be as horrifying as what's imagined, enhancing the psychological impact.

Plot Outline Template

Title: _____

Setting: _____

Theme: _____

Act 1: Setup

• Introduction to Characters: _____

• Inciting Incident: _____

• Establishing Stakes: _____

Key Elements:

• Establish the type of horror

• Initial terrifying conflict

Act 2: The Confrontation

• Deepening Complications: _____

• Midpoint: _____

• Build-Up to Crisis: _____

Key Elements:

• How does the horror evolve or escalate

• The introduction of secondary conflicts or subplots

Act 3: The Resolution

• Climax: _____

• Falling Action: _____

• Denouement/Conclusion: _____

Key Elements:

• Ensure all horrific conflicts are resolved. Stay consistent with the horror

• Highlight how characters have changed

Character Development Sheet

Character Names: _____ / _____

• Nicknames: _____ / _____

• Ages: _____ / _____

• Occupations: _____ / _____

• Physical Descriptions: _____ / _____

• Distinguishing Features (e.g., scars, tattoos):

_____ / _____

Backstory

• Family Background: _____ / _____

• Education & Career Path: _____ / _____

• Significant Past Events: _____ / _____

• Socioeconomic Status: _____ / _____

Personality

• Dominant Traits: _____ / _____

• Fears: _____ / _____

• Desires: _____ / _____

• Hobbies/Interests: _____ / _____

• Habits (good and bad): _____ / _____

• Values & Beliefs: _____ / _____

Relationships

• Current Family Dynamics: _____ / _____

• Friendships: _____ / _____

• Past Romantic Relationships: _____

Goals

• Personal Aspirations: _____ / _____

• Professional Ambitions: _____ / _____

• Romantic Desires: _____ / _____

Conflict

• Internal Conflicts (psychological struggles, fears, uncertainties):

_____

_____

• External Conflicts (with other characters, society, environment):

_____

_____

Character Arc

• Beginning State (personality, situation at the story's start):

_____

_____

• Growth Points (key moments of change):

_____

_____

• End State (transformation or realization by the end):

_____

_____

Dialogue Style

• Speech Patterns (formal, casual, idiosyncratic phrases):

_____ / _____

• Voice (how the character's personality is reflected in dialogue):

_____ / _____

Notes

The Prompt

You discover an unlisted floor between levels of an office building. As you explore, you realize the rooms replicate your deepest fears. Is this real or a hallucination What is your next step?

Gothic Horror

Gothic horror submerges readers into a realm of gloom and deterioration, fusing haunting environments with intricate personalities and heightened emotions. Gloomy castles, ominous weather, and isolated landscapes enhance fear and intrigue. The settings mirror characters' tormented minds, blurring the line between reality and the supernatural. Themes of the past, curses, and forbidden knowledge make gothic horror a rich tapestry of terror and tragedy.

Key Elements:

- Atmospheric Settings: Iconic elements like crumbling mansions, shadowy corridors, and foreboding forests are crucial, setting the tone for the narrative's chilling events.

- Supernatural vs. Psychological: The interplay between overt supernatural occurrences and psychological distress deepens the horror, often leaving characters (and readers) questioning what's real.

- Melodrama and Emotion: Heightened emotions and dramatic interactions underscore the intense personal and moral conflicts faced by characters, adding to the gothic ambiance.

Notable Works and Authors:

1. *Dracula* by Bram Stoker: An ancient vampire stalks the streets of Victorian London, spreading his curse while a group of determined individuals risks everything to stop him.

2. *Frankenstein* by Mary Shelley: A scientist's quest to create life from death results in the birth of a creature that challenges the very notions of humanity and monstrosity.

3. *The Fall of the House of Usher* by Edgar Allan Poe: A man visits his childhood friend in a decaying mansion, only to find himself drawn into a family's legacy of madness and death.

4. *Wuthering Heights* by Emily Brontë: A haunting tale of passionate yet destructive love that transcends life and death, set against the bleak and windswept English moors.

Writing Tips:

- **Leverage the Setting:** Use the setting not just as a backdrop but as an active element of the story that reflects and enhances the psychological and emotional states of the characters.

- **Build Suspense with Revelation:** Gradually reveal the dark secrets of the characters or the setting to build suspense and engage readers through a compelling narrative.

- **Focus on Character Depth:** Develop deeply flawed and morally complex characters whose personal journeys are as compelling as the supernatural elements they encounter.

Plot Outline Template

Title: _____

Setting: _____

Theme: _____

Act 1: Setup

• Introduction to Characters: _____

• Inciting Incident: _____

• Establishing Stakes: _____

Key Elements:

• Establish the type of horror

• Initial terrifying conflict

Act 2: The Confrontation

• Deepening Complications: _____

• Midpoint: _____

• Build-Up to Crisis: _____

Key Elements:

• How does the horror evolve or escalate

• The introduction of secondary conflicts or subplots

Act 3: The Resolution

• Climax: _____

• Falling Action: _____

• Denouement/Conclusion: _____

Key Elements:

• Ensure all horrific conflicts are resolved. Stay consistent with the horror

• Highlight how characters have changed

Character Development Sheet

Character Names: _____ / _____

• Nicknames: _____ / _____

• Ages: _____ / _____

• Occupations: _____ / _____

• Physical Descriptions: _____ / _____

• Distinguishing Features (e.g., scars, tattoos):

_____ / _____

Backstory

• Family Background: _____ / _____

• Education & Career Path: _____ / _____

• Significant Past Events: _____ / _____

• Socioeconomic Status: _____ / _____

Personality

• Dominant Traits: _____ / _____

• Fears: _____ / _____

• Desires: _____ / _____

• Hobbies/Interests: _____ / _____

• Habits (good and bad): _____ / _____

• Values & Beliefs: _____ / _____

Relationships

• Current Family Dynamics: _____ / _____

• Friendships: _____ / _____

• Past Romantic Relationships: _____

Goals

• Personal Aspirations: _____ / _____

• Professional Ambitions: _____ / _____

• Romantic Desires: _____ / _____

Conflict

• Internal Conflicts (psychological struggles, fears, uncertainties):

_____

_____

• External Conflicts (with other characters, society, environment):

_____

_____

Character Arc

• Beginning State (personality, situation at the story's start):

_____

_____

• Growth Points (key moments of change):

_____

_____

• End State (transformation or realization by the end):

_____

_____

Dialogue Style

• Speech Patterns (formal, casual, idiosyncratic phrases):

_____ / _____

• Voice (how the character's personality is reflected in dialogue):

_____ / _____

Notes

The Prompt

A manor is inherited by an art historian, complete with portraits of previous owners who vanished on stormy nights. As a major storm approaches, how does the historian confront the manor's dark past?

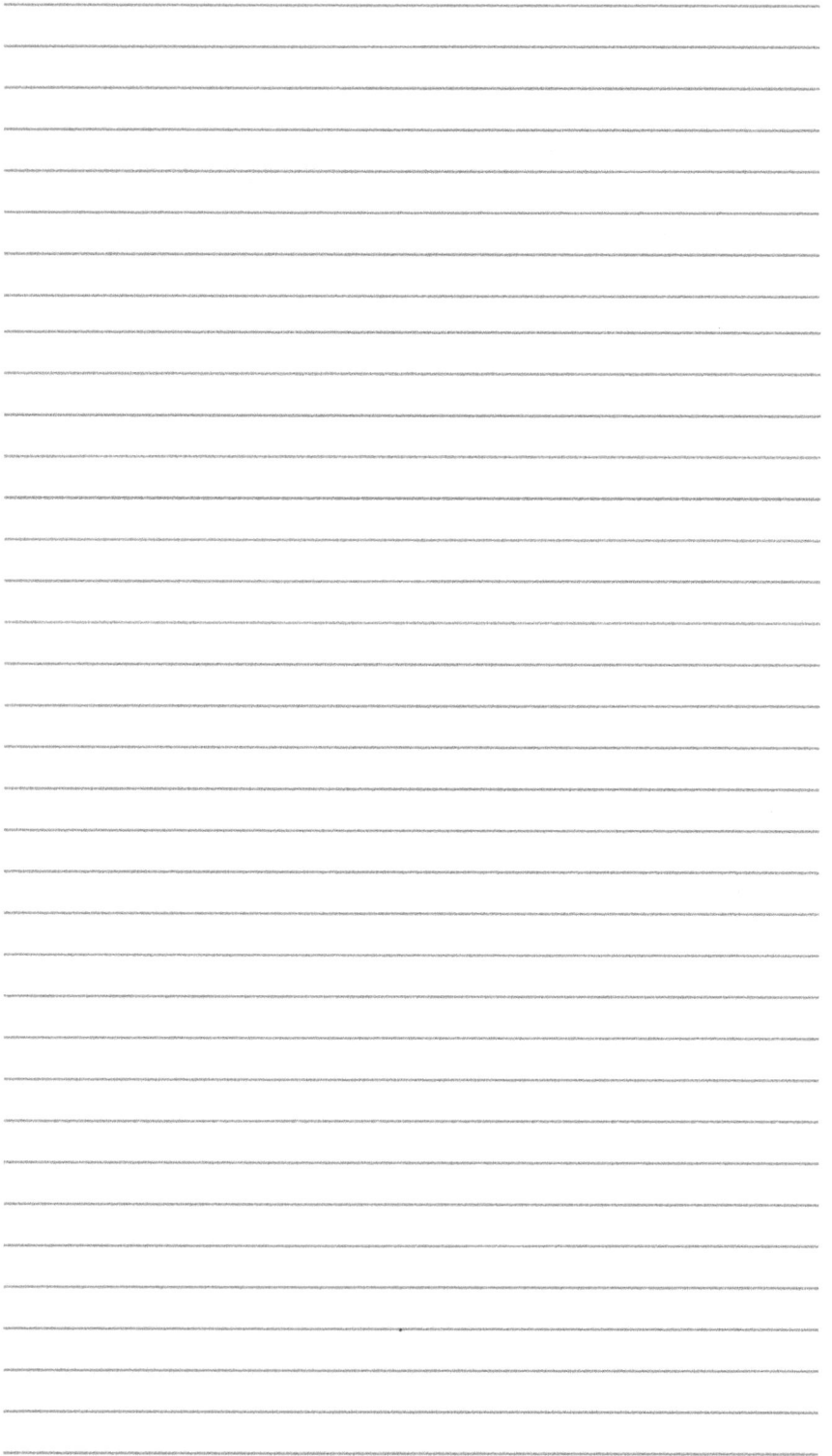

Slasher

Slashers flourish by creating an exhilarating experience of survival, where characters are constantly battling a mysterious and unyielding murderer. This subgenre features heightened suspense, graphic violence, and isolated settings. Slashers examine voyeurism, revenge, and the dark side of human nature, typically through a 'final girl' who confronts the antagonist. The slasher's straightforward scare tactics engage audiences with its chase, escape, and confrontation pattern.

Key Elements:

- Masked Antagonist: The presence of a mysterious and often masked villain adds a layer of intrigue and terror, making the killer both iconic and timeless.

- Isolation: Characters are usually cut off from the outside world, intensifying the sense of danger and limiting their options for escape.

- Survival Instinct: The narrative focuses on the primal fear and suspense of being hunted, highlighting the characters' struggle to outsmart or outlast the killer.

Notable Works and Authors:

1. *The Final Girls Support Group* by Grady Hendrix: A group of women who survived horrific massacres, dubbed "Final Girls," meet regularly to support each other, only to find themselves targeted once again in a deadly plot that forces them to revisit and confront their past traumas.

2. *Off Season* by Jack Ketchum: Set in a remote coastal town, a group of friends encounter a clan of cannibalistic savages. As their peaceful getaway turns into a desperate fight for survival, the boundary between civilization and barbarism blurs.

3. *Clown in a Cornfield* by Adam Cesare: In a fading small town, a new resident, a clown intent on preserving the town's traditional values, turns homicidal at a high school party, targeting the town's youth in a bloody rampage that tests the limits of community and survival.

4. *Ex-Boogeyman* by Kristopher Triana: A former horror movie slasher icon, now retired and facing obscurity, finds his murderous instincts reignited when real-life copycat killings start mirroring his films, pulling him into a dark world he thought he had left behind.

Writing Tips:

- **Maintain High Tension:** Keep the pacing tight and the stakes high to maintain suspense and engage your audience continuously.

- **Develop the Antagonist:** Give your killer a backstory that intrigues and terrifies, adding depth to the horror and motivations behind their actions.

- **Craft Resourceful Characters:** While victims in slasher stories often face grim odds, creating clever and resourceful characters can make for a more engaging and unpredictable story.

Plot Outline Template

Title: _____

Setting: _____

Theme: _____

Act 1: Setup

• Introduction to Characters: _____

• Inciting Incident: _____

• Establishing Stakes: _____

Key Elements:

• Establish the type of horror

• Initial terrifying conflict

Act 2: The Confrontation

• Deepening Complications: _____

• Midpoint: _____

• Build-Up to Crisis: _____

Key Elements:

• How does the horror evolve or escalate

• The introduction of secondary conflicts or subplots

Act 3: The Resolution

• Climax: _____

• Falling Action: _____

• Denouement/Conclusion: _____

Key Elements:

• Ensure all horrific conflicts are resolved. Stay consistent with the horror

• Highlight how characters have changed

Character Development Sheet

Character Names: _____ / _____

• Nicknames: _____ / _____

• Ages: _____ / _____

• Occupations: _____ / _____

• Physical Descriptions: _____ / _____

• Distinguishing Features (e.g., scars, tattoos):

_____ / _____

Backstory

• Family Background: _____ / _____

• Education & Career Path: _____ / _____

• Significant Past Events: _____ / _____

• Socioeconomic Status: _____ / _____

Personality

• Dominant Traits: _____ / _____

• Fears: _____ / _____

• Desires: _____ / _____

• Hobbies/Interests: _____ / _____

• Habits (good and bad): _____ / _____

• Values & Beliefs: _____ / _____

Relationships

• Current Family Dynamics: _____ / _____

• Friendships: _____ / _____

• Past Romantic Relationships: _____

Goals

• Personal Aspirations: _____ / _____

• Professional Ambitions: _____ / _____

• Romantic Desires: _____ / _____

Conflict

• Internal Conflicts (psychological struggles, fears, uncertainties):

_____

_____

• External Conflicts (with other characters, society, environment):

_____

_____

Character Arc

• Beginning State (personality, situation at the story's start):

_____

_____

• Growth Points (key moments of change):

_____

_____

• End State (transformation or realization by the end):

_____

_____

Dialogue Style

• Speech Patterns (formal, casual, idiosyncratic phrases):

_____ / _____

• Voice (how the character's personality is reflected in dialogue):

_____ / _____

Notes

The Prompt

Alumni receive mysterious messages at their high school reunion, followed by horrifying deaths of former classmates. Trapped by a storm, they must uncover a dark past event to find the killer before it's too late.

Body Horror

Body horror explores the visceral terror associated with the transformation, mutation, or destruction of the human body. This subgenre highlights fears of bodily violation and disintegration, with graphic depictions of physical change. By exploring infection, disease, and metamorphosis, body horror exposes the fragility and adaptability of the human form. It examines the unsettling connection between biology and horror, triggering fears of losing control.

Key Elements:

- Transformation and Mutation: Central to body horror is the graphic and often grotesque transformation of bodies, whether through disease, genetic anomalies, or mysterious afflictions.

- Loss of Identity: As characters undergo physical changes, they often experience a corresponding loss of personal or human identity, enhancing the horror of their situation.

- Visceral Imagery: Graphic depictions of the body's alteration are used to evoke fear and disgust, challenging the viewer's comfort with their own physicality.

Notable Works and Authors:

1. *The Metamorphosis* by Franz Kafka: A man awakens one morning to find himself inexplicably transformed into a grotesque insect, alienating him from his family and leading him into a crisis of identity and existence.

2. *The Fly* by George Langelaan: A scientist experimenting with matter transportation accidentally merges his body with that of a fly, leading to horrific consequences as he gradually loses his human traits.

3. *The Strange Case of Dr. Jekyll and Mr. Hyde* by Robert Louis Stevenson: A scientist creates a potion that unleashes his darker self, transforming him physically and mentally into a monstrous figure, embodying the dual nature of man.

4. *The Troop* by Nick Cutter - On a remote island, a scout troop encounters a horrifyingly thin and hungry stranger who harbors a bioengineered nightmare. The boys must survive as they are exposed to a horrifying parasite that causes gruesome and uncontrollable mutations, testing their sanity and humanity.

Writing Tips:

- **Detail Physical Changes:** Emphasize the details of the physical transformation to capture the horror of the body's betrayal of the self.

- **Explore Psychological Impact:** Focus on the psychological ramifications of bodily changes to deepen the narrative and engage with themes of identity and humanity.

- **Use Symbolism:** Incorporate symbolic elements to enrich the story, using the body as a metaphor for broader themes like societal decay, personal change, or the fear of the unknown.

Plot Outline Template

Title: _____

Setting: _____

Theme: _____

Act 1: Setup

• Introduction to Characters: _____

• Inciting Incident: _____

• Establishing Stakes: _____

Key Elements:

• Establish the type of horror

• Initial terrifying conflict

Act 2: The Confrontation

• Deepening Complications: _____

• Midpoint: _____

• Build-Up to Crisis: _____

Key Elements:

• How does the horror evolve or escalate

• The introduction of secondary conflicts or subplots

Act 3: The Resolution

• Climax: _____

• Falling Action: _____

• Denouement/Conclusion: _____

Key Elements:

• Ensure all horrific conflicts are resolved. Stay consistent with the horror

• Highlight how characters have changed

Character Development Sheet

Character Names: _____ / _____

• Nicknames: _____ / _____

• Ages: _____ / _____

• Occupations: _____ / _____

• Physical Descriptions: _____ / _____

• Distinguishing Features (e.g., scars, tattoos):

_____ / _____

Backstory

• Family Background: _____ / _____

• Education & Career Path: _____ / _____

• Significant Past Events: _____ / _____

• Socioeconomic Status: _____ / _____

Personality

• Dominant Traits: _____ / _____

• Fears: _____ / _____

• Desires: _____ / _____

• Hobbies/Interests: _____ / _____

• Habits (good and bad): _____ / _____

• Values & Beliefs: _____ / _____

Relationships

• Current Family Dynamics: _____ / _____

• Friendships: _____ / _____

• Past Romantic Relationships: _____

Goals

• Personal Aspirations: _____ / _____

• Professional Ambitions: _____ / _____

• Romantic Desires: _____ / _____

Conflict

• Internal Conflicts (psychological struggles, fears, uncertainties):

_____

_____

• External Conflicts (with other characters, society, environment):

_____

_____

Character Arc

• Beginning State (personality, situation at the story's start):

_____

_____

• Growth Points (key moments of change):

_____

_____

• End State (transformation or realization by the end):

_____

_____

Dialogue Style

• Speech Patterns (formal, casual, idiosyncratic phrases):

_____ / _____

• Voice (how the character's personality is reflected in dialogue):

_____ / _____

Notes

The Prompt

A well-known tattoo artist realizes his latest ink has unusual effects on clients' behavior and physicality. How does he confront this horrifying revelation?

Zombie Horror

Zombie horror is so compelling because it tells stories of the undead returning to haunt the living, often acting as a chilling symbol for epidemics, societal collapse, or the most primal aspects of human nature. This subgenre mixes survival horror and apocalyptic themes, emphasizing the fight of the living to uphold their humanity and society amidst relentless zombie hordes. Zombie horror explores fear, survival, and ethics through infection, transformation, and gruesome confrontations.

Key Elements:

- The Undead Threat: Zombies are the central horror element, often depicted as relentless and driven by a singular desire to consume the living, which heightens the tension and fear.

- Survival and Desperation: The narrative often centers on the survival strategies of the protagonists, portraying a desperate battle against overwhelming odds where resourcefulness and group dynamics are key.

- Social Commentary: Zombie tales delve into deeper themes, commenting on contemporary issues through horror.

Notable Works and Authors:

1. *World War Z* by Max Brooks: A global perspective on a zombie apocalypse, chronicling different survival stories and strategies from various cultures and countries, reflecting on the international response to a worldwide threat.

2. *The Girl with All the Gifts* by M.R. Carey: In a post-apocalyptic future, a young girl who is both human and infected holds the key to understanding the zombie condition, challenging the remnants of humanity to reconsider what it means to be alive.

3. *Zone One* by Colson Whitehead: Set in a post-apocalyptic New York, survivors work to clear 'Zone One' of remaining zombies, exploring themes of memory, loss, and the attempt to rebuild society amidst constant fear.

4. *Feed* by Mira Grant: In a world where people have adapted to a constant threat of zombies, bloggers uncover a conspiracy during a presidential campaign, highlighting the role of media and technology in a fear-driven society.

Writing Tips:

- **Emphasize the Horrific and the Mundane:** Balance scenes of intense zombie horror with moments of everyday survival to create a relatable and immersive world.

- **Develop Compelling Characters:** Flesh out your characters with backstories and depth, making their struggles and choices in the apocalypse emotionally impactful.

- **Incorporate Varied Perspectives:** Show different societal reactions and personal responses to the zombie threat to add complexity and realism to the narrative.

Plot Outline Template

Title: _____

Setting: _____

Theme: _____

Act 1: Setup

• Introduction to Characters: _____

• Inciting Incident: _____

• Establishing Stakes: _____

Key Elements:

• Establish the type of horror

• Initial terrifying conflict

Act 2: The Confrontation

• Deepening Complications: _____

• Midpoint: _____

• Build-Up to Crisis: _____

Key Elements:

• How does the horror evolve or escalate

• The introduction of secondary conflicts or subplots

Act 3: The Resolution

• Climax: _____

• Falling Action: _____

• Denouement/Conclusion: _____

Key Elements:

• Ensure all horrific conflicts are resolved. Stay consistent with the horror

• Highlight how characters have changed

Character Development Sheet

Character Names: _____ / _____

• Nicknames: _____ / _____

• Ages: _____ / _____

• Occupations: _____ / _____

• Physical Descriptions: _____ / _____

• Distinguishing Features (e.g., scars, tattoos):

_____ / _____

Backstory

• Family Background: _____ / _____

• Education & Career Path: _____ / _____

• Significant Past Events: _____ / _____

• Socioeconomic Status: _____ / _____

Personality

• Dominant Traits: _____ / _____

• Fears: _____ / _____

• Desires: _____ / _____

• Hobbies/Interests: _____ / _____

• Habits (good and bad): _____ / _____

• Values & Beliefs: _____ / _____

Relationships

• Current Family Dynamics: _____ / _____

• Friendships: _____ / _____

• Past Romantic Relationships: _____

Goals

• Personal Aspirations: _____ / _____

• Professional Ambitions: _____ / _____

• Romantic Desires: _____ / _____

Conflict

• Internal Conflicts (psychological struggles, fears, uncertainties):

_____

_____

• External Conflicts (with other characters, society, environment):

_____

_____

Character Arc

• Beginning State (personality, situation at the story's start):

_____

_____

• Growth Points (key moments of change):

_____

_____

• End State (transformation or realization by the end):

_____

_____

Dialogue Style

• Speech Patterns (formal, casual, idiosyncratic phrases):

_____ / _____

• Voice (how the character's personality is reflected in dialogue):

_____ / _____

Notes

The Prompt

In a zombie-infested world, a radio DJ broadcasting from an underground station becomes a beacon of hope. Upon receiving a cure signal, choose between pursuing it or supporting survivors through broadcasts.

Cosmic Horror

Cosmic horror, frequently linked to the writings of H.P. Lovecraft, explores the fear stemming from the unknown and the unfathomable powers that exist beyond human comprehension. This subgenre portrays humans as insignificant in the vast cosmos, confronting them with ancient, powerful entities beyond human understanding. Cosmic horror stories evoke existential dread and fear of a strange, hostile, and indifferent universe.

Key Elements:

- Incomprehensible Entities: Central to cosmic horror are beings or forces that are beyond the scope of human understanding, whose presence challenges the very fabric of reality.

- Sense of Insignificance: Characters often face situations that make them feel utterly powerless and trivial in the grand scheme of the universe, enhancing the existential themes of the genre.

- Atmosphere of Dread: Unlike traditional horror that might rely on jump scares or visible monsters, cosmic horror builds an overwhelming atmosphere of dread and foreboding through the unknown.

Notable Works and Authors:

1. *At the Mountains of Madness* by H.P. Lovecraft: An Antarctic expedition uncovers strange fossils and a lost alien city, revealing horrifying secrets about the origins of life and a previous civilization that challenges the sanity of its discoverers.

2. *The Ballad of Black Tom* by Victor LaValle: In 1920s New York, a street musician is drawn into a plot involving a mysterious book that reveals a reality too terrible to comprehend, facing cosmic horrors and racial prejudices.

3. *Revival* by Stephen King: A preacher loses his faith and turns to experiments that touch on electrical powers to harness what lies beyond death, leading to terrifying revelations about what comes after life.

4. *Annihilation* by Jeff VanderMeer: A team of scientists explores a mysterious, mutating landscape known as Area X, which defies all attempts to understand it and alters all who enter in profound and disturbing ways.

Writing Tips:

- **Focus on the Unknown:** Keep the true nature of the cosmic entities vague to maintain a sense of mystery and terror.

- **Create a Mood of Desolation:** Use settings and descriptions that emphasize isolation and detachment to enhance the otherworldly and existential themes.

- **Portray Psychological Impact:** Show how encounters with the incomprehensible affect the minds and behaviors of characters, often leading to madness or transformation.

Plot Outline Template

Title: _____

Setting: _____

Theme: _____

Act 1: Setup

• Introduction to Characters: _____

• Inciting Incident: _____

• Establishing Stakes: _____

Key Elements:

• Establish the type of horror

• Initial terrifying conflict

Act 2: The Confrontation

• Deepening Complications: _____

• Midpoint: _____

• Build-Up to Crisis: _____

Key Elements:

• How does the horror evolve or escalate

• The introduction of secondary conflicts or subplots

Act 3: The Resolution

• Climax: _____

• Falling Action: _____

• Denouement/Conclusion: _____

Key Elements:

• Ensure all horrific conflicts are resolved. Stay consistent with the horror

• Highlight how characters have changed

Character Development Sheet

Character Names: _____ / _____

• Nicknames: _____ / _____

• Ages: _____ / _____

• Occupations: _____ / _____

• Physical Descriptions: _____ / _____

• Distinguishing Features (e.g., scars, tattoos):

_____ / _____

Backstory

• Family Background: _____ / _____

• Education & Career Path: _____ / _____

• Significant Past Events: _____ / _____

• Socioeconomic Status: _____ / _____

Personality

• Dominant Traits: _____ / _____

• Fears: _____ / _____

• Desires: _____ / _____

• Hobbies/Interests: _____ / _____

• Habits (good and bad): _____ / _____

• Values & Beliefs: _____ / _____

Relationships

• Current Family Dynamics: _____ / _____

• Friendships: _____ / _____

• Past Romantic Relationships: _____

Goals

• Personal Aspirations: _____ / _____

• Professional Ambitions: _____ / _____

• Romantic Desires: _____ / _____

Conflict

• Internal Conflicts (psychological struggles, fears, uncertainties):

_____

_____

• External Conflicts (with other characters, society, environment):

_____

_____

Character Arc

• Beginning State (personality, situation at the story's start):

_____

_____

• Growth Points (key moments of change):

_____

_____

• End State (transformation or realization by the end):

_____

_____

Dialogue Style

• Speech Patterns (formal, casual, idiosyncratic phrases):

_____ / _____

• Voice (how the character's personality is reflected in dialogue):

_____ / _____

Notes

The Prompt

An ancient text summons a cosmic entity that warps reality. As the world starts to crumble, there must be a way to reverse the summoning without losing sanity. What are the methods to stop the madness?

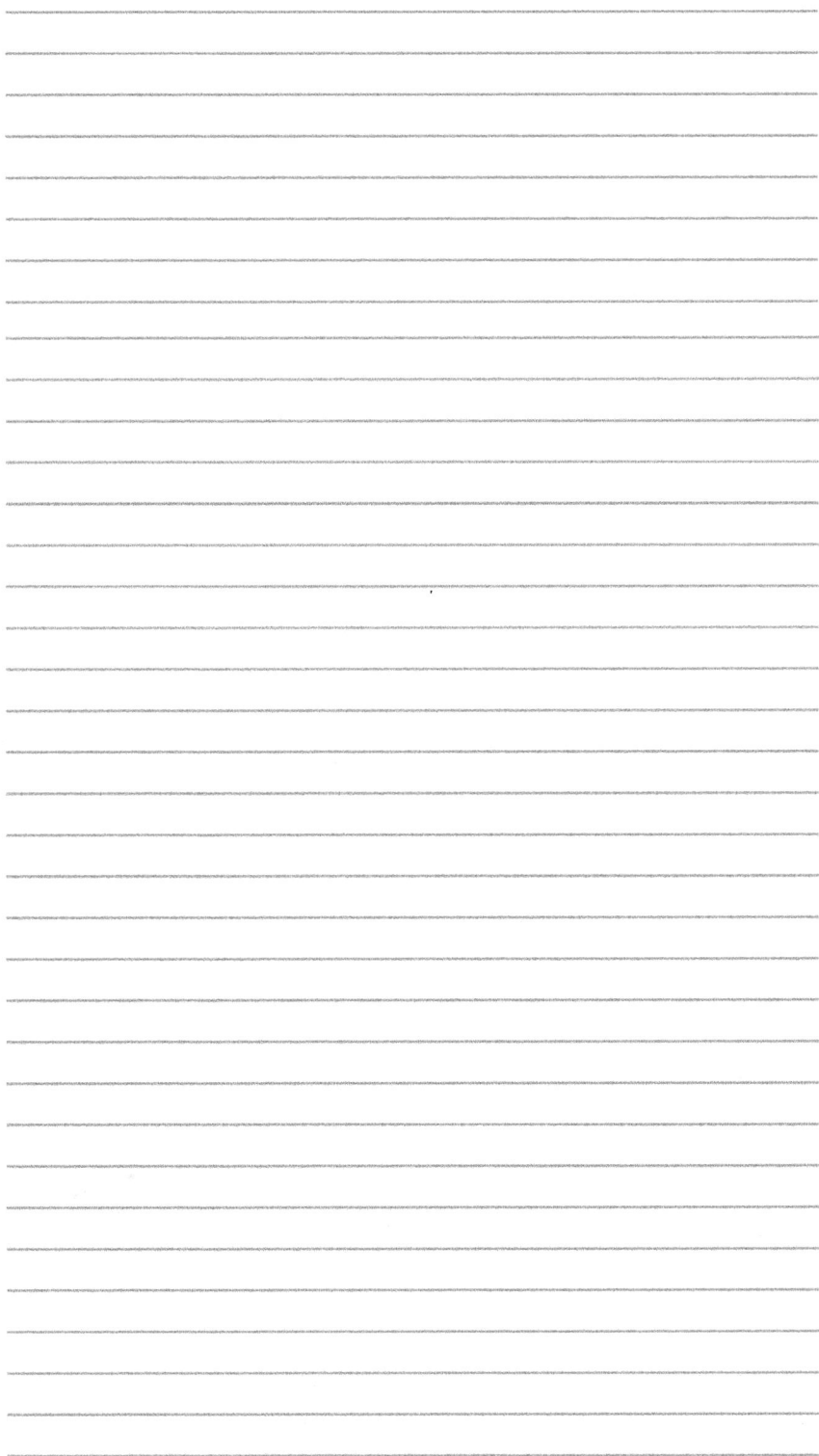

Survival Horror

Survival horror focuses on the protagonist's struggle to endure in threatening environments. This subgenre blends horror elements with intense, sometimes suffocating survival situations that test the characters' physical and mental boundaries. It's about persevering through impossible obstacles when trapped or isolated in dangerous conditions.

Key Elements:

- Hostile Environment: Characters are often placed in extreme settings whether it's a desolate wasteland, a merciless jungle, or a locked-down biohazard facility, that test their survival skills to the maximum.

- Resource Scarcity: The constant scarcity of essential resources, such as food, water, weapons, or safe shelter, adds to the tension and forces characters to make perilous decisions.

- Psychological Strain: The continuous stress of the situation leads to intense psychological and emotional pressure, revealing the characters' deepest fears and the human capacity for both resilience and despair.

Notable Works and Authors:

1. *The Road* by Cormac McCarthy: In a post-apocalyptic world, a father and his young son journey across a barren America that is devoid of life and hope, facing the remnants of humanity gone savage to protect each other and keep the concept of hope alive.

2. *Bird Box* by Josh Malerman: In a world where seeing the outside can drive you insane, a mother blindfolds herself and her children to make a perilous journey to what she hopes will be safety.

3. *The Mist* by Stephen King: After a mysterious mist envelops a small town, trapping the residents inside a supermarket, the survivors must fend off creatures hidden in the fog while grappling with the collapse of social order.

4. Grimeweave by Tim Curran: In the dark jungles of Indochina, a monstrous ancient evil awaits in a forgotten valley. Michael Spiers, a Marine sniper and sole survivor of a previous encounter, reluctantly joins a Force Recon team to hunt this stealthy, bloodthirsty creature.

Writing Tips:

- **Emphasize the Environment:** Use detailed descriptions to create a vivid and oppressive atmosphere that enhances the sense of danger and claustrophobia.

- **Develop Strong Character Arcs:** Characters should evolve in response to the trials they face, showcasing human resilience and the psychological impacts of their struggle.

- **Balance Action with Reflection:** While survival horror thrives on high-stakes scenarios, moments of reflection deepen the emotional resonance and allow for tension to build.

Plot Outline Template

Title: _____

Setting: _____

Theme: _____

Act 1: Setup

• Introduction to Characters: _____

• Inciting Incident: _____

• Establishing Stakes: _____

Key Elements:

• Establish the type of horror

• Initial terrifying conflict

Act 2: The Confrontation

• Deepening Complications: _____

• Midpoint: _____

• Build-Up to Crisis: _____

Key Elements:

• How does the horror evolve or escalate

• The introduction of secondary conflicts or subplots

Act 3: The Resolution

• Climax: _____

• Falling Action: _____

• Denouement/Conclusion: _____

Key Elements:

• Ensure all horrific conflicts are resolved. Stay consistent with the horror

• Highlight how characters have changed

Character Development Sheet

Character Names: _____ / _____

• Nicknames: _____ / _____

• Ages: _____ / _____

• Occupations: _____ / _____

• Physical Descriptions: _____ / _____

• Distinguishing Features (e.g., scars, tattoos):

_____ / _____

Backstory

• Family Background: _____ / _____

• Education & Career Path: _____ / _____

• Significant Past Events: _____ / _____

• Socioeconomic Status: _____ / _____

Personality

• Dominant Traits: _____ / _____

• Fears: _____ / _____

• Desires: _____ / _____

• Hobbies/Interests: _____ / _____

• Habits (good and bad): _____ / _____

• Values & Beliefs: _____ / _____

Relationships

• Current Family Dynamics: _____ / _____

• Friendships: _____ / _____

• Past Romantic Relationships: _____

Goals

• Personal Aspirations: _____ / _____

• Professional Ambitions: _____ / _____

• Romantic Desires: _____ / _____

Conflict

• Internal Conflicts (psychological struggles, fears, uncertainties):

_____

_____

• External Conflicts (with other characters, society, environment):

_____

_____

Character Arc

• Beginning State (personality, situation at the story's start):

_____

_____

• Growth Points (key moments of change):

_____

_____

• End State (transformation or realization by the end):

_____

_____

Dialogue Style

• Speech Patterns (formal, casual, idiosyncratic phrases):

_____ / _____

• Voice (how the character's personality is reflected in dialogue):

_____ / _____

Notes

The Prompt

A storm leaves a cruise ship stranded on a remote island overrun with feral creatures. Struggling without resources, they must adapt quickly to escape the island's deadly new inhabitants. Do they make it out alive?

Folk Horror

Folk horror explores the unsettling customs and deep-seated fears that originate from rural settings and close-knit societies. This subgenre highlights the clash between tradition and modernity, including pagan rituals and dark folklore. Folk horror exposes the terror of ancient customs and beliefs, often with deadly consequences. The genre highlights the clash between rationality and mystical forces that govern forgotten ways of life.

Key Elements:

- Rural and Isolated Settings: Settings are typically secluded villages or dense forests that are steeped in history and superstition, enhancing the feeling of being cut off from the modern world.

- Ancient Rituals and Curses: The narrative often revolves around old rituals, curses, or folklore that resurface in the present, bringing horror to those who encounter or unwittingly unleash them.

- Atmosphere of Dread: Folk horror builds a profound sense of dread through the landscape and its connection to the supernatural or arcane practices, making the setting itself a character that embodies ancient terror.

Notable Works and Authors:

1. *The Wicker Man* by Robin Hardy and Anthony Shaffer (adapted from their screenplay): A police sergeant is sent to a Scottish island village in search of a missing girl whom the townsfolk claim never existed. He finds himself enmeshed in the island's terrifying pagan practices.

2. *Harvest Home* by Thomas Tryon: A family moves to a small New England town only to find that the community's idyllic facade conceals sinister and ancient rituals centered around the harvest.

3. *The Ritual* by Adam Nevill: Four old university friends reunite for a hiking trip in the Scandinavian wilderness, only to stumble upon an ancient evil that stalks them through the forest.

4. *The Loney* by Andrew Michael Hurley: When a pilgrimage to a shrine on a desolate stretch of the English coastline reveals the darkness within each pilgrim and the secrets of the land, the faith of a group is severely tested by the terrifying forces they uncover.

Writing Tips:

- **Leverage the Landscape:** Use the natural environment to create an eerie setting that enhances the story's supernatural elements.

- **Incorporate Local Lore:** Weave local myths or folklore into the narrative to give the horror a sense of authenticity and rootedness in the setting.

- **Explore Social Dynamics:** Focus on the dynamics within small communities or isolated groups, highlighting how ancient customs can clash with individual desires or modern sensibilities.

Plot Outline Template

Title: _____

Setting: _____

Theme: _____

Act 1: Setup

• Introduction to Characters: _____

• Inciting Incident: _____

• Establishing Stakes: _____

Key Elements:

• Establish the type of horror

• Initial terrifying conflict

Act 2: The Confrontation

• Deepening Complications: _____

• Midpoint: _____

• Build-Up to Crisis: _____

Key Elements:

• How does the horror evolve or escalate

• The introduction of secondary conflicts or subplots

Act 3: The Resolution

• Climax: _____

• Falling Action: _____

• Denouement/Conclusion: _____

Key Elements:

• Ensure all horrific conflicts are resolved. Stay consistent with the horror

• Highlight how characters have changed

Character Development Sheet

Character Names: _____ / _____

• Nicknames: _____ / _____

• Ages: _____ / _____

• Occupations: _____ / _____

• Physical Descriptions: _____ / _____

• Distinguishing Features (e.g., scars, tattoos):

_____ / _____

Backstory

• Family Background: _____ / _____

• Education & Career Path: _____ / _____

• Significant Past Events: _____ / _____

• Socioeconomic Status: _____ / _____

Personality

• Dominant Traits: _____ / _____

• Fears: _____ / _____

• Desires: _____ / _____

• Hobbies/Interests: _____ / _____

• Habits (good and bad): _____ / _____

• Values & Beliefs: _____ / _____

Relationships

• Current Family Dynamics: _____ / _____

• Friendships: _____ / _____

• Past Romantic Relationships: _____

Goals

• Personal Aspirations: _____ / _____

• Professional Ambitions: _____ / _____

• Romantic Desires: _____ / _____

Conflict

• Internal Conflicts (psychological struggles, fears, uncertainties):

_____

_____

• External Conflicts (with other characters, society, environment):

_____

_____

Character Arc

• Beginning State (personality, situation at the story's start):

_____

_____

• Growth Points (key moments of change):

_____

_____

• End State (transformation or realization by the end):

_____

_____

Dialogue Style

• Speech Patterns (formal, casual, idiosyncratic phrases):

_____ / _____

• Voice (how the character's personality is reflected in dialogue):

_____ / _____

Notes

The Prompt

A documentary filmmaker explores a village's festival with dark origins. What sinister secrets will come to light as the festival draws near, and how will the filmmaker respond to the unfolding horror?

Eco-Horror

Eco-horror explores the horrifying outcomes of human intervention in the natural world, highlighting themes of environmental devastation and the monstrous repercussions that can arise. In this subgenre, nature is depicted as rising up against humanity's mistreatment of the environment, with plants, animals, or the earth itself seeking retribution. Eco-horror taps into fears of pollution, climate change, and species extinction, showing nature's wrath when pushed too far.

Key Elements:

- Nature's Retaliation: Nature retaliates with rampaging animals, aggressive plant life, and catastrophic disasters caused by humans.

- Human Hubris and Exploitation: Characters often include those whose actions have harmed the environment, providing a critical look at the consequences of ecological exploitation and the moral questions surrounding human responsibility.

- Atmosphere of Imminent Threat: Eco-horror builds suspense and terror through the looming threat of nature's unpredictable and often violent responses, creating a constant sense of impending doom.

Notable Works and Authors:

1. *The Swarm* by Frank Schätzing: The world's marine life starts to behave in strange and aggressive ways, leading to global catastrophes as scientists discover an unknown intelligence beneath the sea, provoked to wrath by human activities.

2. *Annihilation* by Jeff VanderMeer: A team of scientists explores Area X, a mysterious and mutating landscape that defies biological understanding, reflecting nature's bizarre new adaptations in response to environmental damage.

3. *The Ruins* by Scott Smith: A group of tourists becomes trapped on a Mexican hillside where aggressive vines and plants not only trap but actively hunt them, revealing the horrifying potential of the natural world when it turns hostile.

4. *The Hungry Tide* by Amitav Ghosh: Set in the Sundarbans mangroves, this story explores human life coexisting with dangerous wildlife, where environmental changes provoke increasingly aggressive encounters between humans and animals.

Writing Tips:

- **Highlight Ecological Themes:** Integrate real-world environmental issues into the horror narrative to ground the story in reality and enhance its relevance.

- **Develop the Setting as a Character:** Treat the environment itself as a dynamic character, one that reacts vividly and violently to human actions.

- **Focus on Psychological Impact:** Explore the psychological terror and guilt experienced by characters who face the wrath of nature as a consequence of their own or society's actions.

Plot Outline Template

Title: _____

Setting: _____

Theme: _____

Act 1: Setup

• Introduction to Characters: _____

• Inciting Incident: _____

• Establishing Stakes: _____

Key Elements:

• Establish the type of horror

• Initial terrifying conflict

Act 2: The Confrontation

• Deepening Complications: _____

• Midpoint: _____

• Build-Up to Crisis: _____

Key Elements:

• How does the horror evolve or escalate

• The introduction of secondary conflicts or subplots

Act 3: The Resolution

• Climax: _____

• Falling Action: _____

• Denouement/Conclusion: _____

Key Elements:

• Ensure all horrific conflicts are resolved. Stay consistent with the horror

• Highlight how characters have changed

Character Development Sheet

Character Names: _____ / _____

• Nicknames: _____ / _____

• Ages: _____ / _____

• Occupations: _____ / _____

• Physical Descriptions: _____ / _____

• Distinguishing Features (e.g., scars, tattoos):

_____ / _____

Backstory

• Family Background: _____ / _____

• Education & Career Path: _____ / _____

• Significant Past Events: _____ / _____

• Socioeconomic Status: _____ / _____

Personality

• Dominant Traits: _____ / _____

• Fears: _____ / _____

• Desires: _____ / _____

• Hobbies/Interests: _____ / _____

• Habits (good and bad): _____ / _____

• Values & Beliefs: _____ / _____

Relationships

• Current Family Dynamics: _____ / _____

• Friendships: _____ / _____

• Past Romantic Relationships: _____

Goals

• Personal Aspirations: _____ / _____

• Professional Ambitions: _____ / _____

• Romantic Desires: _____ / _____

Conflict

• Internal Conflicts (psychological struggles, fears, uncertainties):

_____

_____

• External Conflicts (with other characters, society, environment):

_____

_____

Character Arc

• Beginning State (personality, situation at the story's start):

_____

_____

• Growth Points (key moments of change):

_____

_____

• End State (transformation or realization by the end):

_____

_____

Dialogue Style

• Speech Patterns (formal, casual, idiosyncratic phrases):

_____ / _____

• Voice (how the character's personality is reflected in dialogue):

_____ / _____

Notes

The Prompt

Mutated sea creatures terrorize a small coastal town due to experimental pesticide runoff. How do the townspeople respond to the horror and what sacrifices are needed to restore balance?

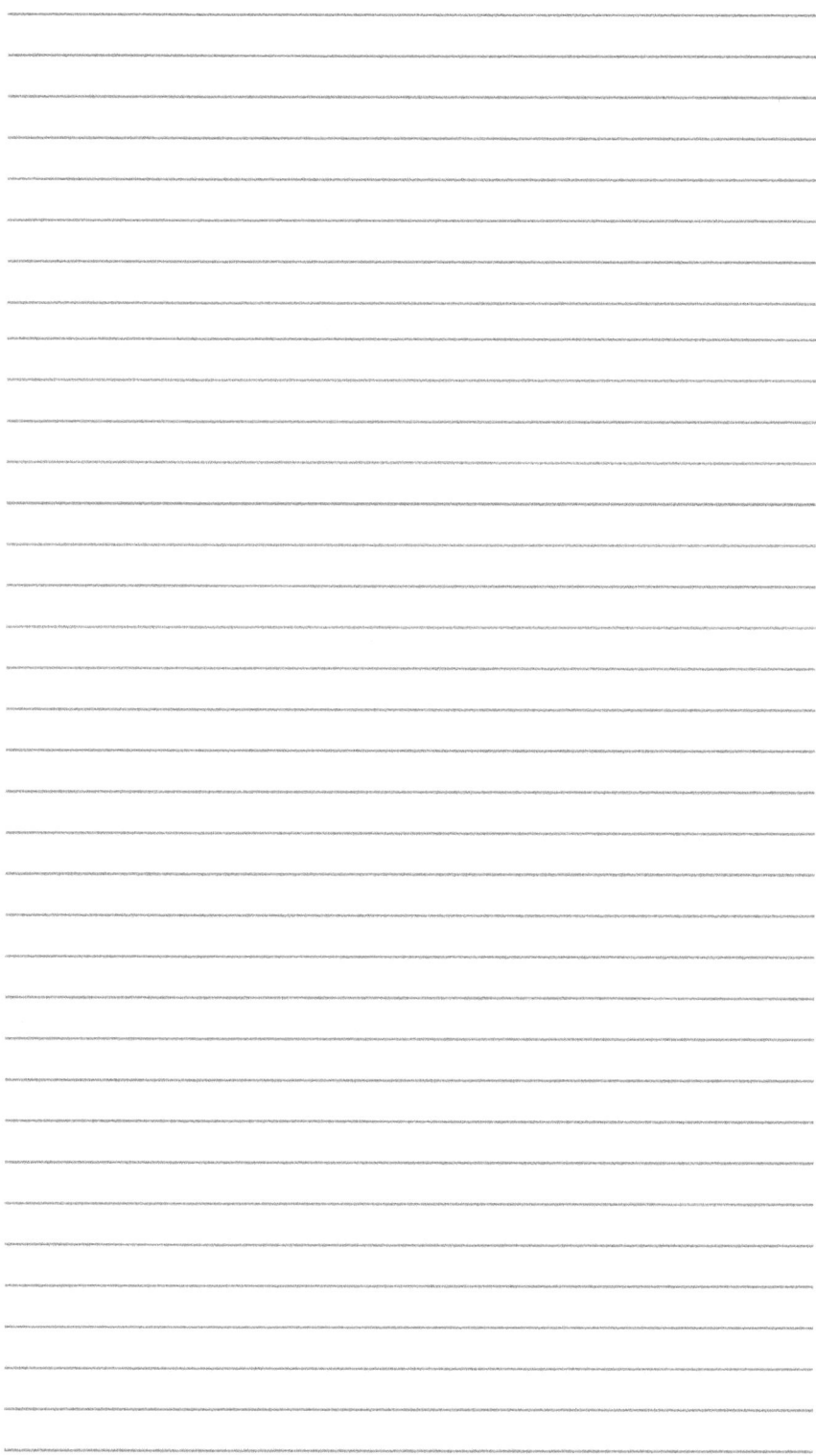

Thank You!

As we reach the end of our journey together through these prompts, I hope you've found sparks of inspiration, moments of challenge, and above all, a deeper love for the art of storytelling. If this book has played a part in your writing journey, I invite you to share your experience by leaving a review.

Your insights not only celebrate our shared passion for storytelling but also guide fellow writers to resources that could enlighten their own creative paths. Whether it's a brief note or an in-depth reflection, your feedback is a beacon for the community and a treasure for me.

Thank you for embracing the adventure of writing with me. Your engagement and support illuminate the way forward.

With warmest regards,

Mark El-Ayat

STORY PROMPTS

This book is one in a series that features various genres of story prompts. Take your creative journey to the next level with our Story Prompts books. They're designed to inspire and guide your storytelling across various genres.

Find new worlds, interesting characters, and exciting plots that are waiting for your unique voice.

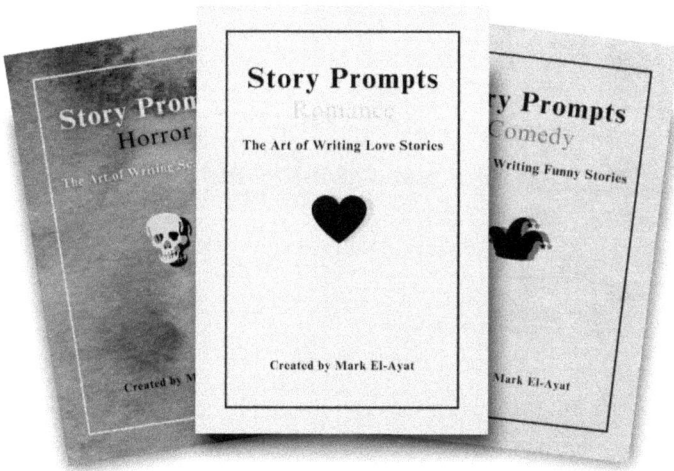

Our Story Prompts series is here to help writers at any stage, with a wide range of prompts to dive into different themes, characters, and plots. Don't stop writing! Your next amazing story starts right here!

For more information and to discover other books in the series, visit my website www.markelayat.com

www.ingramcontent.com/pod-product-compliance
Lightning Source LLC
Chambersburg PA
CBHW052116030426
42335CB00025B/3012